Basic Skills
Summarizing

Focusing on Main Ideas and Details and Restating in Concise Form

Grades 5-6

by
Norm Sneller

Published by Instructional Fair
an imprint of
Frank Schaffer Publications®

Instructional Fair

Author: Norm Sneller
Editors: Mary Hassinger, Wendy Roh Jenks, Sara Bierling
Cover Artist: Laura Zarrin

Frank Schaffer Publications®

Instructional Fair is an imprint of Frank Schaffer Publications.

Send all inquiries to:
Frank Schaffer Publications
8720 Orion Place
Columbus, OH 43240-2111

Summarizing—grades 5-6

ISBN: 0-7424-0107-3

12 13 14 15 PAT 12 11 10 09

About the Book

Summarizing is the skill of comprehending, focusing on important information, and rephrasing that information in a concise form. *Summarizing* for grades 5–6 contains guided activities that help develop and achieve this skill. Students will progress from selecting main ideas and details to writing their own summaries. As this skill is practiced in reading, students will naturally begin to use the skill in writing and speaking. Summarization is a concept used throughout the curriculum. Social studies, science, language, and reading all use the skill of summarization in written, read, and oral lessons.

This book provides activities that will give students the opportunity to discuss, examine, choose, and write summaries. It will also provide the chance to practice using active verbs, and colorful, interesting nouns in their work.

Table of Contents

Uncle Bob's Zoo

Uncle Bob loves animals. While he cannot afford to care for live animals, he has created a computer library of his favorites. Here are the texts for three of his pets.

Dolphins

These carnivorous ocean-dwelling mammals live in coastal waters, bays, and lagoons around the world. With keen hearing, they are capable of detecting noises at frequencies up to seven times those detectable by humans. Dolphins harvest fish using their built in sonar, or echolocation. They make clicking noises underwater and decipher the location of their prey by the returning sound waves that bounce off objects. A group of dolphins is known as a pod. Scientists consider this creature to be among the most intelligent of all animal life.

Baboons

These omnivorous land-loving primates are found in parts of Africa and Arabia. They prefer life on the ground to the tree-climbing life of their cousins, the monkey. They are easily identified by their long faces, overhanging brows, and their colorful, hairless backsides. They have a good sense of smell and eat small mammals, crustaceans, insects, and other tiny crawling creatures. They also feed on plants and fruit. One baboon species, the *gelada*, grazes the grasslands for its nourishment. Baboons have large cheek pouches in which they can store their food for easy travel. A group of baboons is called a troop and may range in number from 30 to 100 members.

Squirrels

These primarily herbivorous rodents can be found in all parts of the world except Australia and Antarctica. All but the ground squirrel live in trees. They differ from one another in size. The pygmy squirrel of Africa may stretch to five inches (13 cm) in length, while the giant squirrel of Asia can easily grow to a 36 inch (90 cm) length. They love to eat buds, seeds, and nuts, but often will feast on insects. Squirrels help spread trees and other plants throughout the countryside by scattering and storing seeds. Different subfamilies may be red, brown, gray, or blue. The woolly flying squirrel with a body and a tail each 2 feet (30 cm) long was thought to be extinct until it was rediscovered in the Himalayan Mountains.

Uncle Bob's Zoo (cont.)

Match the details below with each of the animals. Cross off the three details that match none of the animals.

carnivore	echolocation	good sense of smell
flying	herbivore	howler
live in trees	long faces	no tail
ocean-dwelling	omnivore	land-loving
pods	related to cat	rodent
store seeds	troop	very intelligent

Dolphins   Baboons   Squirrels

_____   _____   _____

_____   _____   _____

_____   _____   _____

_____   _____   _____

Write a one-sentence summary of the differences between these three animals.

_____

_____

_____

Simply Put

Read the three paragraphs below. Circle the best summary for each article.

Charles De Gaulle became a brigadier general early in the Second World War. When the German army advanced and France fell to them, he escaped to London. There he formed a French national committee in exile. With this body he was able to organize the French resistance. Together with other exiled Frenchmen, De Gaulle joined the British to conquer Syria.

1. Which of these sentences best summarizes the article above?

   a. Charles De Gaulle was known for his stubborn determination.
   b. Charles De Gaulle was a French general and leader during World War II.
   c. During World War I Charles De Gaulle was wounded three times and taken prisoner by the Germans.

Erwin Rommel led the Seventh Tank Division as the German forces dashed across the French countryside on their way to the English Channel. Because his moves were so brilliant as commander of the *Afrika Korps* in North Africa, his friends and enemies called him the Desert Fox. Knowing that the Allied forces would likely attack along the English Channel, the Germans made Rommel responsible for the German defense of Northern France in 1944. After the invasion, Rommel was accused by other German officers of participation in the attempted assassination of Hitler in July. In response, Erwin Rommel killed himself.

2. Which of these sentences best summarizes the article above?

   a. Rommel escaped North Africa in 1943 shortly before the Afrika Korps's defeat.
   b. Rommel was a part of the assassination plot against Adolf Hitler.
   c. Erwin Rommel was a famous German soldier who, despite his great military accomplishments, was accused of plotting Hitler's assassination.

Bernard Montgomery was appointed commander of the British Eighth Army in Africa. Although the German army had earlier success there, "Monty" began the offensive at Al 'Alamayn in Egypt, which successfully forced the German and Italian soldiers out. When General Eisenhower became supreme commander of the Allied forces, Montgomery served as the chief of the British forces. In August of 1944, he was promoted to field marshal of British and Canadian troops.

3. Which of these sentences best summarizes the article above?

   a. Bernard Montgomery served his country in its war against Germany and Italy during the Second World War.
   b. General Montgomery was an ardent supporter of General Eisenhower.
   c. Bernard Montgomery was responsible for ridding North Africa of the German troops.

 Name _____

In Conclusion

Study the three graphs below, then summarize the information.

Sheep Production of East Ada, Nova Scotia (*Each sheep represents 1000 head.*)

1. Summarize the findings of the chart above.

_____

Bear Claw Ice Cream Production (*Each paw represents 5,000 liters of ice cream sold.*)

1980

1982

1984

1986

2. Summarize the findings of the chart above.

_____

Boys Named Osh Kosh Gene along the Wisconsin/Illinois Corridor
(*Each figure represents ten boys.*)

| 1790 | 1800 | 1810 | 1820 |

3. Summarize the findings of the chart above.

_____

Bon Appetit!

For a writing exploratory, Shanelle chose to write a recipe. Here is her project.

Recipe for Completing 6th Grade

1. Be kind to others.
2. Sleep enough at night.
3. Avoid bullies, gossips, and tattletales.
4. Don't get caught running in the hall.
5. Organize your time.
6. Do not become the teacher's pet.
7. Memorize the names of the countries of Africa and Asia.
8. Read more of the newspaper than just the sports section.
9. Get your school work done.
10. Learn to write well.

Answer these questions using complete sentences.

1. What is a summary of Shanelle's list?

   _____

2. Which of her detail(s) could relate to the social studies curriculum?

   _____

   _____

3. Which of the rules above are negative statements?

   _____

   _____

4. Take one of the ten details. Explain in a simple narrative why Shanelle may have included it. Use no more than three sentences.

   _____

   _____

   _____

Name _____

Whoa!

(Read the recipe below and answer the questions that follow.)

Feeling adventurous, a pair of youths entered Don Pablo's Spicy Restaurant where they ordered hamburgers topped with Don Pablo's special steak sauce. Below is the Don's secret recipe.

---

1 part black pepper	2 parts black mustard
1 part allspice	1 part dill
0.5 part cloves	4 parts red pepper
1 part fennel	

3 parts Corinthian brand ketchup (B4 Steak Sauce may be substituted.)

Directions: Finely chop all ingredients and mix thoroughly into the ketchup. Always have a glass of water handy when you try Don Pablo's steak sauce.

---

1. What would you expect this sauce to do for you?

_____

2. Which ingredient is used most in this recipe?

_____

3. In a simple summary, write a one-sentence advertisement for this product.

_____

4. Don Pablo will include 3 grams of cloves in his next batch. Calculate how much of the other ingredients he will need to include?

_____	black pepper	_____	black mustard
_____	allspice	_____	dill
_3 g_	cloves	_____	red pepper
_____	fennel	_____	ketchup

SPICES

What's Going On?

Match these summary statements with the articles below.

____ 1. When we help others selflessly, we allow ourselves to grow emotionally.

____ 2. One's fears may often seem irrational.

____ 3. Sights, tastes, or smells may trigger memories of past experiences.

____ 4. In emergencies we perform feats we might otherwise consider impossible.

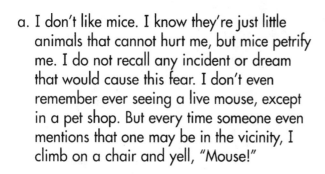

a. I don't like mice. I know they're just little animals that cannot hurt me, but mice petrify me. I do not recall any incident or dream that would cause this fear. I don't even remember ever seeing a live mouse, except in a pet shop. But every time someone even mentions that one may be in the vicinity, I climb on a chair and yell, "Mouse!"

b. On his way to school Mark, saw the puppy. He heard it, too, as it whined and pulled against its choke chain. The small cocker spaniel was shaking with fear, its chain caught in the fence links, pulling tighter and tighter around its neck. When it saw Mark, the puppy barked, but couldn't move. So Mark spoke to it in a comforting, soothing voice. He slowly reached in to untangle the puppy's chain, and gently held the little one near to his chest. It whined and sniffled and cuddled and then reached up to lick Mark's chin. Although he figured he'd be late for school, Mark knocked on apartment-house doors until he found the puppy's owner. The

old woman's gratitude did Mark's heart good.

c. There it was again—that burning smell. It was unlike any other odor Terry had ever smelled—not burning leaves nor plastic; not the stench of burnt rubber nor the reek of singed hair; not the pungent camp fire smell, either. No, the scent was similar to that of the smoky mist when ... hmm ... that night when the Norton's old Five and Dime store burned to the ground downtown. What a sight that had been, Terry mused. Boy! That must have happened fifteen or twenty years ago!

d. Dale smiled as he watched his baby nephew Jackson crawl across the grassy yard. What a mover! Along the back of the yard rested an old car on cinder blocks, its tires gone. The baby crawled toward this rusting hulk, slowly reached for the door handle, and pulled himself up. Suddenly the ancient car lurched and slipped off the blocks, knocking the startled child to the ground. The baby's

What's Going On? (cont.)

cry stirred something inside Dale. He dashed across the yard. Without hesitation, he lifted the side of the car, called for help, and held the vehicle aloft until others arrived and removed the screaming child.

5. Write an article or story for the following summary statement: Although people want what they don't have, once they have it, they don't care for it anymore.

_____

_____

_____

_____

11

Matchmaker

Match each set of detail sentences in the left column with
its summary statement in the box to the right.

____1. • The children groaned when we woke them so
    early.
  • My wife brought a blanket to sit on the ground.
  • The sun appeared over the treetops.
  • It was a magnificent sight to see.

____2. • This activity teaches responsibility and caring for
    others.
  • Limited space is needed to raise rabbits.
  • Raising rabbits is an excellent opportunity to
    teach economics to children.
  • There is a good market for the sale of
    domesticated rabbits.

____3. • We arrived at the gates before the park opened.
  • The weather stayed cool and sunny all day long.
  • Our whole family rode every ride they wanted
    without having to wait in long lines.
  • The animal exhibition showcased interesting and
    exotic animals of the world.

____4. • Mom spent three hours preparing lasagna for dinner.
  • Dad kept opening the saucepan and sampling the sauce.
  • All six of us had two helpings of lasagna.
  • There were no leftovers to freeze for lunches.

____5. • Tadas carefully laid out a plan for each section of his garden.
  • The hardware store where he bought gardening supplies was very crowded.
  • It took five days to fully prepare the garden plot.
  • Tadas weeds the garden every Saturday morning.

____6. • People were waiting in line for tickets all night.
  • Fans of the band Torch were willing to pay $100 a ticket.
  • This performance would be attended by more people than any other in this stadium.
  • Tickets for the concert were sold out in less than two hours.

a. Having a garden can be
   very time consuming.

b. Raising rabbits is a valuable
   experience for children.

c. Torch is a very popular
   band.

d. This year's vacation to the
   amusement park was lots of
   fun.

e. The new lasagna recipe was
   a hit with the whole family.

f. The sunrise my family experienced was spectacular.

I Plant

Read the poem and answer the questions below.

I have planted a memory tree,
neither too great
nor too small.
A tree for life,
to celebrate the beauty around me
and to remind me.

May this tree of life I have set to earth
grow roots strongly anchored,
grow branches stretching wide,
to remind me often
of a grandparent's arms
and that loving embrace.

1. Write a summary of the poet's message.

_____

_____

2. What does the poet remember?

_____

_____

3. What is the poet celebrating?

_____

_____

4. Which word is a synonym for secured? _____

5. Which words show the poet is joyful?

_____

Puppy Love

> Read the poem below. Answer the questions using complete sentences.

My owner is the very best,
She pets and plays and all the rest.
I get the best food in my dish,
She's kinder than I'd ever wish.
I'd never put her to the test.

She loves me true, all of the time.
Even with coat covered in grime.
Of course, there are times that she scolds,
But I'm never left out in the cold.
Her love knows no reason or rhyme.

Even as we both grow up
And I'm no longer just a pup,
She hugs and plays and talks to me.
I know two friends we'll always be,
Even when we're both grown up.

1. Summarize the message.

_____

2. Name four things the dog loves about its life.

_____

3. What word is a synonym for dirt? _____

4. What does "knows no reason or rhyme" mean?

_____

The Gang's All Here

The Fun Club has five members. They motivate one another with interesting and fun competitions. Study the chart illustrating one of their activities, then answer the questions.

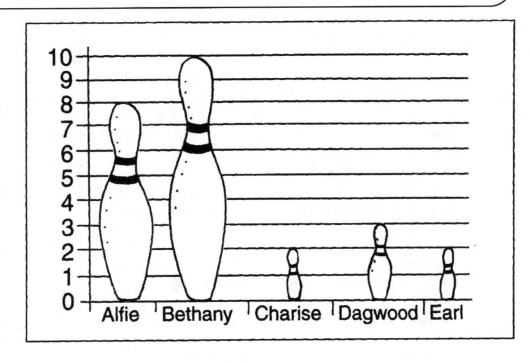

1. How might you summarize the club's bowling?

   _____

2. Who had the lowest score?

   _____

3. Whose pin average was best?

   _____

4. What is the group's average?

   _____

5. What suggestions would you make to the club?

   _____

Into the West

Read the story and answer the questions below.

A Native American people of the western United States, the Shoshoni, currently number about 10,000 people. While many now live on one of three reservations, for many years they traveled through the mountains and valleys of Idaho, Montana, Utah, Wyoming, and Nevada in search of food.

They believed in a creator god named Duma Appa'h. According to legends, this god heard the people's morning prayer, which was carried heavenward on the rays of the sun.

Although Appa'h was the great creator of the Earth, the animal nation assisted him with other creations. For example, according to legend, Coyote made humans.

A group of mystical beings was the Nunumbi, or Little People, who, when angered by humans, might shoot them with invisible arrows.

The Shoshoni may be a small family of Americans, but their stories should be told and remembered.

1. Write a summary of the ancient Shoshoni religious beliefs.

   _____

2. How many people are part of the Shoshoni tribe today?

   _____

3. Which word in the text above is a synonym for supernatural?

   _____

4. According to the old beliefs, how did prayers reach Appa'h?

   _____

5. What are three other cultural groups you might wish to explore?

   _____

Challenge: Choose one of the groups you listed in #5. Write a short essay, including:

   1. where they live   2. how many members today
   3. their beliefs   4. other features

Mine Eyes Have Seen

The following is a brief explanation of how the human eye sees. Read the explanation, then answers the questions below.

Reflected light

Cornea and Pupil

Brain

EYE

Retina: Rods and Cones

Lens

a. Reflected light enters the eye through the cornea and pupil.

b. This light image is focused with the help of the lens.

c. The image is projected upside-down on a "screen" called the retina.

d. On the retina are cones which distinguish color, light, and detail. These cones are especially useful for day vision. They send information to the brain by way of the optic nerve.

e. Also on the retina are rods which distinguish motion and objects. These rods are very important for night vision. They, too, send information to the brain by way of the optic nerve.

f. A person has 20/20 vision if he sees at 20 feet what a normal-visioned person sees at 20 feet. A person with 20/200 vision sees at 20 feet what a normal-visioned person sees at 200 feet.

1. Summarize how we receive sight.

    _____

2. Define the word distinguish. _____

3. What do we call the eye's screen? _____

4. What part of the eye is most important for day vision? _____

5. What part of the eye is most important for night vision? _____

6. What does it mean to have 20/80 vision?

    _____

7. What does it mean to have 40/20 vision?

    _____

Man in Space

Read this time line showing important dates in the life of Charles Conrad, Jr.
Then answer the questions below.

1930	born in Philadelphia
1953	graduated from Princeton University
1953	entered Navy; completed Navy test for pilot school
1962	became an astronaut
1965	piloted the Gemini 5 mission
1966	commanded the Gemini 11 mission
1969	commanded the Apollo 12 flight; landed module on moon
1973	served as commander of the first mission of Skylab
1974	retired from both Navy and astronaut program
1999	died in motorcycle accident

1. Write a simple summary of the life of Charles Conrad.

_____

2. When did Conrad first become an astronaut? _____

3. In what year did he land on the moon? _____

4. For how many years did he serve in the Navy? _____

5. Which program came first: Apollo, Gemini, or Skylab?

_____

Name _____

Peeves

Read the cartoon carefully, then answer the questions below.

1. Summarize the situation presented.

   _____

2. Why was the teacher, Mr. Boomer, upset?

   _____

3. What kind of classroom is this? _____

4. Circle the adjectives that best describe the student, Ben.

   wise   hopeful   confused   noisy   bashful

5. Finish this sentence.

   Because Ben mistook his teacher's comment, the teacher ...

   _____.

A Polaroid Moment

Read the cartoon, then answer the questions below.

1. Which of the following best summarizes the cartoon?

   a. A father lovingly pushes his daughter on a swing.

   b. A daughter blames her father for his accidental wipe out.

   c. A father swings his daughter and pays a dear price.

2. In this cartoon, what is meant by an underdog?

   _____

3. How does the artist portray the girl's happiness?

   _____

4. Write three words that mean the same as joy. _____,_____,_____

5. Why might the mother take a picture of this scene?

   _____

6. Write an optional title for this comic strip.

   _____

Name _____

 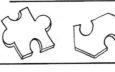

Does it Fit?

Read the four summary statements below. Then read the eighteen detail sentences. Match each with a summary sentence, using letters A, B, C, or D.

Summary A: A young wolf experiences her first success as a hunter.

Summary B: An alien creature discovers that many Earthlings enjoy potato chips.

Summary C: The city of Minneapolis has a bustling night life.

Summary D: With effort, an elderly man hopes to prove he is self-sufficient.

_____ 1. Wherever you go, streets are filled with moving cars and busy people.

_____ 2. In the grey-blue predawn, the pup sniffed the air excitedly against the scent of game.

_____ 3. Slowly his trusty Lincoln rolled into the traffic lane, the driver gripping the wheel firmly.

_____ 4. He watched as many "two-leggers" placed peculiar flakes into their face openings and made crunching and smacking sounds.

_____ 5. She returned to her den, meat in mouth, head and tail held high in victory!

_____ 6. He stepped out of the house and painstakingly bypassed the sheet of ice on his stoop.

_____ 7. It dashed about in the open tundra startling small creatures gathering food.

_____ 8. You rush into the nightclub hoping you're not too late for the premier act.

_____ 9. There, at a wooden platform, sat humans holding shiny blue bags in one hand, and pulling flake-like yellowish white bits from a bag.

_____ 10. Joining the theatergoers, you swarm into the auditorium, eager to hear the latest dramatic work.

_____ 11. The large flakes are being used to scoop a thick white substance from bowls.

_____ 12. Suddenly Xlevty's scanner wildly chattered as Earthlings everywhere loudly pounced upon those flakes, grabbed them, and shoveled them into their head cavities.

_____ 13. Barking and snarling, the canine leaped upon an unsuspecting grouse.

_____ 14. Squinting his eyes to see better, he read the label on the cans of vegetables in Aisle 5.

_____ 15. In a busy restaurant, you compete with others for the waiter's attention.

_____ 16. Xlevty perked up his audio scanner and asked himself, "What is that crunching sound?"

_____ 17. With trembling hands, he picked up the electric razor and stared into the mirror.

_____ 18. He sighed as he checked his mailbox for the license renewal.

Mystery of the Disappearing Lunches

Growing up with five brothers wasn't easy. For one thing, they have a tendency to completely overwhelm you—with the noise level, the sports equipment, the testing out of new wrestling moves. Another downside is that nothing is just yours. It seems like brothers believe "what's mine is mine and what's yours is mine."

It really shouldn't have surprised me when my school lunches started disappearing from the refrigerator each morning. Mom was so good to us, preparing the six bag lunches each evening. But when I went to grab mine on Monday it was gone! And it was gone every day for a week! Of course, Mom questioned all of the boys and each one denied taking my lunch. It wasn't so difficult to make another one, but it was annoying! After a week of this, Mom had us make our own lunches, thinking that if we packed our own it would be reasonable to believe that we would pack what we wanted and not need more.

Unfortunately, this didn't work. Besides having an incredible mess in the kitchen every evening and huge amounts of food going into the lunch bags, mine was still missing in the morning. Ready to do anything, Mom finally decided to consult Dad. She had been trying not to bother him with too many problems since he had been working so many overtime hours, but this was getting increasingly frustrating. Should she ground all the boys? Should she just give me lunch money?

As Mom told Dad about the situation at the dinner table that night, with all of us sitting there eating, Dad actually blushed a little! The boys burst out laughing when Dad said with a little chuckle, "Oh, weren't one of those lunches meant for me? I thought you were saving me time by packing mine, too, especially since I've been leaving at five in the morning."

With the mystery of my missing lunches solved and Mom's promise to make Dad his own lunch, my brothers were off the hook. That is until my nail polish started disappearing.

Answer the following using complete sentences.

1. Write a brief summary of the story. Put events in sequential order.

_____

2. How does the author feel about her brothers? Why do you say this?

_____

3. Write another possible solution to the mystery of the disappearing lunches. Be brief but complete.

_____

4. Create another title for this story.

_____

A Dirty Deal

> Read the letter, then answer the questions that follow.

42 Current Ave.
Howell, MI 48843
February 12, 2000

Dear Sir or Madam,

Last fall I purchased your much publicized video game *MudFight*. In your television commercials you claim that this game would have you "eat dirt until you hurt." I must tell you I hurt, because buying this game was as bad as eating dirt.

First, the package arrived late. I ordered it over the Internet on the fifth of October, and it did not arrive until December 4, well past the five-day delivery guarantee.

Second, the game has not produced the sounds of slurping mud, croaking frogs, Tarzan's yodel, nor the wails of sliding victims mentioned in the television commercials. The only sounds I hear are buzzing bees, chattering monkeys, and waddling ducks. Sounds like false advertising to me.

Third, every time my hero makes it safely to the Frog Prince's Lily Pad—you know, the one at Level 4 just beyond the Ravin' Rabbit Hole—the game freezes up.

Finally, last Tuesday, the game caused a meltdown of my entire entertainment system. I was entering a cave I discovered in Level 7 not far from Mud Monkey's Lair when the screen became wavy. A text frame filled the screen which read, "Got You, Dirt Bag!" Fifteen seconds later, smoke came pouring out of the disc port. Because I lost my entire system, I request two things of you. The first is reimbursement for the game *MudFight* at $55.94 (tax + shipping/handling charges). The second is a down payment toward the purchase of a new GamePort Entertainment System at $294.95.

With Chagrin,

Jack Dram

1. Which of these statements best summarizes the intent of the letter?
   a. A buyer wishes to congratulate a company for keeping true to its promise.
   b. A buyer wishes to return a game that failed to meet expectations.
   c. A buyer wishes to receive money for a program which was faulty.

2. What are the four complaints of the writer?
   a. _____
   b. _____
   c. _____
   d. _____

It's a Party

Below is an invitation to Annie's birthday party.
Read carefully and answer the following questions using complete sentences.

Hey Girls!
It's Party Time!

Come on
and join
the fun!

You're Invited to a Pizza Party!

For: Annie Thorp

When: Friday, March 4, 5:30 pm

Where: 912 Aimsworth Drive

Why: To celebrate Annie's birthday!

R.S.V.P: Tuesday, March 1

            Do not bring gifts!

1. Summarize the purpose of this card.

   _____

2. What does R.S.V.P. mean? (You may want to research this to give the French meaning.)

   _____

3. Why do you think the card states no gifts?

   _____

4. Using a sheet of drawing paper, design a card of your own. Include all of the information Annie

   included in hers.

Back Me Up, Guys!

Read the summaries and statements below. Put an X by the statements that do not give supporting details to the summaries.

1. A dragonfly prepares itself for flight and obtains its food.

_____a. Sighting a mosquito, the dragonfly soared toward the creature and captured it with its basket of six legs.

_____b. A blue jay spotted the insect flying below and cried raucously.

_____c. It lifted and swooped over the river's water in search of food.

_____d. Because of the misty morning, the dragonfly fanned its wings, drying them in the sun's light.

_____e. As it continued its flight, the dragonfly ate its fresh meal.

_____f. Dragonflies may be red, black, blue, or green in color.

2. A mink escapes a ranch by diving into a river.

_____a. The mature American mink may grow to 20 inches (50 cm) in length.

_____b. Chased by a mink farm worker, it dove into the cold November water of the Pine River.

_____c. The mink swam swiftly downstream and upon reaching a pile of brush, lifted its head above water to see if its enemy had followed.

_____d. The fox searched for food, which included mink, squirrel, and bird eggs.

_____e. The young mink squeezed through the wire mesh of the pen.

_____f. The mink was protected from the frigid water by its two layers of fur.

Write four statements that support the following summary.

3. The sunrise was the most beautiful thing he had ever experienced.

a. _____

b. _____

c. _____

d. _____

I Like Ike

Read the following article. Then answer
the questions on page 27.

Len was given the assignment of researching and writing a brief report about Dwight D. Eisenhower's military career. Read his report and answer the following questions.

Dwight David Eisenhower, whose real name was David Dwight Eisenhower, was born in Texas, in 1890. Besides being the 34th President of the United States of America, Eisenhower had a brilliant military career. His more than thirty years of military discipline, leadership, and responsibility prepared him for his two terms as president. Called "Ike" by people throughout the world, he was well-respected by citizens and world leaders.

Although Eisenhower's family practiced pacifism, he was encouraged by friends to attend the military academy at West Point, where he received a higher education and military training. After graduation in 1915, he began his military career in earnest, quickly going from second lieutenant to first lieutenant in the United States Army. He was on the staff of such great leaders as Brigadier General Fox Conner and General Douglas MacArthur. While serving as MacArthur's aide in the Philippines, he planned the Philippine military defense and helped in organizing a military academy for their newly-formed independent country.

When World War II began, and the United States began to feel it might become involved in that European battle, Eisenhower earned a promotion to brigadier general. By March 1942, after serving in the Army's war plan division, he was promoted to major general, and in June of 1942 was named commanding general of the United States forces in the European Theater of Operations. By 1943, Eisenhower was promoted to four-star general, then the highest rank in the Army at that time.

His military abilities so impressed the leaders of the United States, including President Franklin Delano Roosevelt, that Eisenhower was named supreme commander of the Allied Expeditionary Forces in Europe. In this position, he orchestrated the armies and navies of the United States, Great Britain, and other Allied nations, to work together to protect the world from total German invasion. The infamous battle at Normandy, on June 6, 1944, took place under Eisenhower's command.

Even after the German surrender in May of 1945, Eisenhower continued his work for the United States Army. As a five-star general, he was named Army chief of staff in November, 1945—a position he held until his temporary retirement in 1948. With the formation of NATO in 1949, Eisenhower was appointed supreme commander of NATO forces in Europe in 1950. He remained in this position until his Republican nomination for the presidency, a position he held for two full terms.

I Like Ike (cont.)

Answer the questions using the article on page 26.

1. Briefly summarize Eisenhower's military career. Write facts in sequential order, according to the report.

_____

_____

_____

_____

2. List six different military positions Eisenhower held in the United States Army.

_____

_____

_____

3. Using the dates given in the essay, make a timeline below showing the progress of Eisenhower's military career.

_____

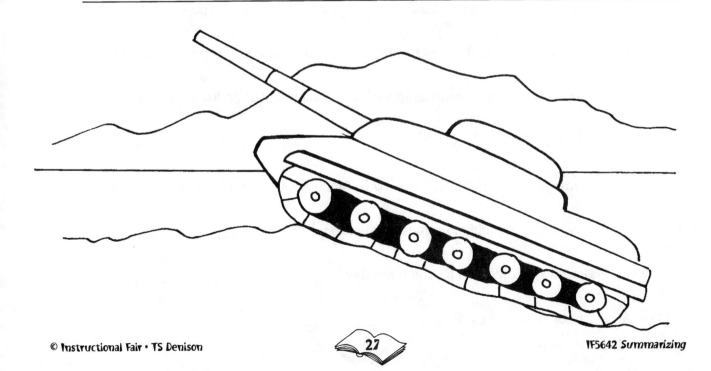

The Real Babe

> Read this time line which highlights a part of Babe Didrikson Zaharias' life.
> Then answer the questions below.

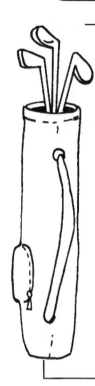

1914	born in Port Arthur, Texas
1932	won gold medals in the Olympics in track and field
1938	married George Zaharias
1946	won the U.S. Amateur Championship in golf
1949	became a founding member of the Ladies Professional Golf Association
1950	named by the AP poll "the greatest woman athlete of the first half of the 20th Century"
1951	won her fourth world championship in golf
1954	won her final professional tournament, the U.S. Open
1955	published her autobiography
1956	died of cancer

1. Choose the sentence that best summarizes the facts shown above.

   a. To many sports enthusiasts, Babe Didrikson epitomizes the best of sports competition.

   b. Babe Didrikson showed the world what women can accomplish in the world of sports.

   c. Babe Didrikson must be remembered for her accomplishments in track and field.

2. Which came first? Circle one.

   marriage   Olympics   U.S. Amateur Championship title

3. In which sport was she most able to compete professionally? _____

4. Of what organization was Babe a founding member? _____

5. How old was Babe when she died? _____

Family Gathering

Read the selection and answer the questions below.

Seven Sites.
Camping along the shores of the Great Lake.
Seven family groups with tents, campers, cook stoves, bikes, hot dogs, glowing lanterns, coffee pots,
Clotheslines, sun screen, flashlights, bug repellent, swim suits, firewood, canopies, water jugs,
Picnic tables, and the ever present marshmallows.

Sitting in lawn chairs before a fireless pit. Too hot to set the fire. Air too humid to exercise.
Sweat dripping off the tip of the nose. Dreaming of air-conditioned homes and cars.
Where was that lake breeze?

But ears listening to the children.
Games played with cousins seen but once a year.
Questions asked by toddlers too cute to be ignored.
Infant howls through the night.
Songs sung in and out of key.
Bikes skidding along paths searching for greater play.
Elder children anticipating the needs of the young.
Awake and noisy while adults pretend to sleep.
Dashing for the beach for yet another swim.
A human gaggle floating in the freshwater sea in tubes, rafts, life jackets, and swimmies
With ever-cautious adults never far off.

Cousins flitting to and fro, gathering the strands of our varied family groups, greeting each other,
Pulling on our multi-colored strands of loose yarn personalities and braiding us into...one.

1. Write a one-sentence summary of this selection.

   _____

2. How do the children treat each other?

   _____

3. What complaints do the adults have?

   _____

4. What is the greatest benefit of the camping experience to the family? Use the back of this paper to
   write your answer.

Clue Us In

On a rainy Saturday afternoon Tim, Megan, Steve, and Tabitha are sent on a treasure hunt. Read their clues. Then answer the questions on page 31.

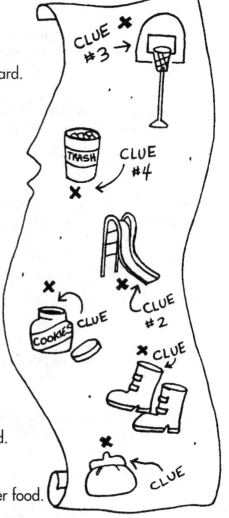

1. Go into the park across the street.
   Under the slide you will see your second clue.

2. You'll find Clue #3, on the back of the north basketball backboard.

3. Don't hold your breath too long!
   Clue #4 is beneath the garbage container.

4. Hungry? Go to Tim's kitchen where you will find a clue
   hidden inside a cookie in the cookie jar.

5. Now check under the sitting room sofa for your next clue.
   I hope this clue is still in one piece!

6. There's a pair of boots at the rear entrance.
   Inside the left boot (near the toe) you'll find your next clue.

7. Dash to Megan's garage.
   Look on the tool table near the window.

8. Check Steve's pants pockets. (Yes, the pants he's wearing!)

9. Now, go to the hutch of the spotted bunny in Megan's backyard.

10. You're getting warm. See if you can get this one:
    think bunny, think Easter. Something in Tabitha's kitchen is Easter food.

11. Good for you! You thought of the egg carton in the fridge. Now, locate
    Santa's dusty destination in Tabitha's living room.

12. Ah ha! (Hopefully you didn't get too dirty from the soot.) Now, see the picture over the mantel?
    Carefully turn it over and...

Prizes found: four coupons for an outing to Mighty Mountain Mini-Golf.

Clue Us In (cont.)

Use page 30 to answer the questions below.

1. Circle the summary of this reading.

    a. Four children reach into a boot for a clue.

    b. Four children have nothing to do on a rainy Saturday afternoon.

    c. Four children read clues in search of a prize.

2. Which clue location might be damaged in the children's search?

    _____

3. What might you assume about Steve, who has a clue hidden inside his pocket?

    _____

4. How long might this treasure hunt take to complete?

    a. 5 minutes

    b. 50 minutes

    c. 5 hours

    d. 50 hours

5. Draw a map of this neighborhood. Include a minimum of four homes with yards and the park. Use the directional rose on the map. The children's homes are located as follows: Tim's is on the southwest side of the neighborhood. Megan lives on the east side. Steve's home is on the southwest corner of the neighborhood, and Tabitha is on the south side.

Name _____

Reactions

A synopsis is a brief outline or summary. Read this synopsis of a play about two students and their adventure in a virtual reality simulation.

Act 1   Airport, early morning

Young Ty Waalkes and his best friend Drew Moore prepare to leave home for the International Scholastic Problem Solvers Finale in Singapore. At the airport, Ty learns that his parents' business, manufacturing solar-powered exhaust fans, is on the edge of bankruptcy. Ty's girlfriend, Gracie, has come to wish him farewell and to inform him that this would be a good time to date other kids. And Ty's kid brother Charlie gruffly informs him that this morning he lost Ty's pet rat. The family bids a fond farewell to the two travelers and wish them well in the tournament.

Act 2   Over the Pacific, early afternoon

Ty and Drew are guided to Concourse G, Gate 54. Here they are informed that the problem-solving simulation will begin momentarily. The boys board what appears to be a Boeing 737 where they are overawed by their fellow "passengers." The man across the aisle constantly pecks away at his laptop and yells into his cell phone. The woman three seats ahead with two children in tow, is returning from the Teenie Tots of the World beauty contest. She angrily rants about cheating judges overlooking her precious jewels. Shortly after take off, a peculiarly secretive elderly woman tries to sell the boys unusual items like jewelry and electronics. During a meal of ham sandwiches and caviar the "passengers" are interrupted by a frantic announcement from the pilot. He informs them that the plane has sucked a flock of unidentified fowl into all four engines and is losing altitude. Suddenly the plane drops.

Act 3   On a life raft in the Pacific, two days later

The simulation continues as Ty awakens on a raft floating out in open sea. He performs first aid on Drew who is still unconscious. They share their raft with Blair, one of the child modeling contestants, the strange elderly woman, an airline steward named Hal who reminds Ty of Barney the Dinosaur, and a fellow student, Chloe, who is also part of the problem solvers competition. As their raftmates' behaviors become increasingly erratic, the three young people take over. They teach the elderly woman and steward how to catch fish and albatross and construct a shelter from the sun using blankets, shirts, and rubber bands provided by Blair. Ty teaches his five mates a song to keep their spirits up. Chloe and the recovered Drew restrain the steward from drowning himself in the shark-infested waters. At dusk, just as their meager water supply runs out, the elderly woman spies land to the southwest.

Reactions (cont.)

Act 4   Singapore harbor, night to dawn

Harbor lights appear in the distance. The raftmates enthusiastically paddle their craft to shore. Upon arrival, the three students learn that the elderly woman is actually a judge for the Problem Solvers Finale. By microphone and hidden camera a team of judges has observed the students from a booth high over the set's ceiling. The audio and video tapes clearly detail the children's progress. Because of their stellar actions, the three win the contest, and they each receive a full college scholarship to a university of their choice. The contest officials arrange to market Ty's parents' product worldwide, thus saving their business. Drew, Chloe, and Ty are interviewed live by all major television networks. Within minutes Ty's girlfriend tearfully calls begging forgiveness. Ty graciously accepts her apologies but agrees she was right. Hand in hand Ty, Chloe, and Drew step from the virtual reality set and greet the setting sun.

1. Write a one- to two-sentence summary of the play.

_____

_____

2. Match each character with the fitting reaction by drawing a line from one column to the other.

    Hal   evaluating

    Drew   tearful

    elderly woman   frantic

    Gracie   diligent

3. What accident caused the plane to plummet?

_____

4. Explain the reward the three contestants received.

_____

_____

5. Imagine you attended the opening of *Reactions*. Give a short review summary of the play on the back of this paper. Be creative but write no more than five sentences.

Name _____

Where, Oh Where?

Read the story and answer the questions on page 35.

I'm a very forgetful person, so it didn't surprise any of my friends when I shouted, "I've lost my science report!"

Paul, Ansil, and Lena all gave suggestions as to possible locations of the report, but one by one they were eliminated. I hadn't stopped at my locker, the girls' gym, the computer lab, or the cafeteria. I even called home, after waiting ten minutes for the pay phone in the main courtyard. Mom was particularly upset, especially since she'd been the one driving me all over town doing research and buying just the right shade of light blue printer paper. She had also done me the huge favor of typing the ten-page report.

"Tara! How could you possibly misplace something so important? Did you check your backpack? Your locker...?" Then she basically repeated my friends' suggestions.

Study hall was over, I had one period left before science, and I was pretty nervous. I had wanted to earn another A in science—it would look so great on my report card—straight A's across the sheet. But this report was a major part of our final grade in Mrs. Hernandez's class. As I sat in geography, mentally retracing my steps and combing my memory for ideas on the report's location, I had a great idea.

I would simply tell Mrs. Hernandez that I had decided to do further research because I was so excited about the subject, and that I hadn't finished typing it the night before. I would tell her that my mother had offered to finish typing it and had broken her finger. I

would just have to come up with some incredible and airtight excuse.

As I slowly wandered toward the science lab, silently rehearsing my excuses, I began to feel guilty. Could I actually look my favorite teacher in the eye and lie about my report? How would I feel then? Maybe worse than I felt when I realized that it was missing.

I tossed my backpack over my shoulder, straightened my back, and walked into the room. Taking a deep breath, I knew what I would do—tell the truth.

I walked up to Mrs. Hernandez's desk to speak with her. As she looked up from the thick stack of papers in front of her, she lightly tapped the top report, a report typed on baby blue paper in a transparent folder.

"Oh, Tara!" said Mrs. Hernandez, "I'm always glad when one or two students hand in these larger reports early. I can really take my time reading them then. Your research on whale migration is incredible. Would you mind sharing with the class?"

I thought I would fall over! How in the world had this happened? All this worrying and waiting...

Where, Oh Where? (cont.)

> Read the story on page 34 carefully, then answer the following questions.

1. What is the main focus of this story? _____

2. The following are sentences that are details from the story. Decide which are needed and which are not. Write *important* or *not important* on the line following each statement.

    a. Tara is a forgetful person. _____

    b. Study hall and geography class are before science. _____

    c. Tara's friends and mother made suggestions on where to find the report. _____

    d. Mrs. Hernandez is the science teacher. _____

    e. At first, Tara was going to lie about the report. _____

    f. Tara decides that telling the truth is best. _____

    g. Mrs. Hernandez already has the report. _____

    h. Tara has no idea how the report got to the teacher. _____

3. In four brief statements, describe what you would do if you lost a major homework assignment.

    _____

    _____

    _____

4. In complete sentences, write your idea of how the report got to Mrs. Hernandez. Be concise in your description. Do not include any unnecessary details. Continue on the back if necessary.

    _____

    _____

Animal Lovers

Read this story about Terrance and Tabitha.
Use the information to fill in the story web on page 37.

Terrance and Tabitha had always loved animals. Even as young children, the twins would rescue hurt or lost creatures while having adventures on the farm. As they grew older, they were more daring and brought the animals to stay in the barn. This went on for years, so when all was said and done, the O'Kelley's had had over one hundred dogs, even more cats and kittens, and an assortment of birds and other animals stay at their home.

Mr. and Mrs. O'Kelley weren't exactly surprised when the twins came to them with a new and wonderful scheme.

"Tabby and I would like to make our animal rescue an official thing. We want to open a sort of animal hospital/hotel," said Terrance. He went on, "We could use the empty side of the main barn. We have it all planned out."

"How will you afford to feed and care for these animals?" Mrs. O'Kelley asked.

That was Tabby's area. "We plan on collecting cans for recycling, and asking the kids at school to do the same. Then they can come out here and help care for them and play with them. It'll be their reward for doing the can collecting."

"That's how we plan on taking care of the animals, especially when we get a bunch," said Terrance. "We can have the kids out for a swim in the pond and an hour or two in the barn with the animals."

Dad had a question. "What about the animals that really need medical attention? How do you plan on paying Dr. Wong for checking them out? And what about the others

that we don't recognize and have some illness we can't even guess at? That could be dangerous, kids!"

"We've already talked to Dr. Wong. He agreed that this is a great idea. He's even willing to volunteer two hours one afternoon a week checking out the animals, if we help him on Saturday mornings. All we have to do is clean out the four kennels he has at the office. We know how to do that, since we do it for our own animals, so it's just not a problem," explained Tabitha. "Dr. Wong also has three larger cages we can have to keep really sick or ornery animals in until he comes."

Mr. and Mrs. O'Kelley looked at each other. Mom smiled and said, "Well, you two have certainly done your homework. Why don't you go outside and let your father and me talk about this. We'll tell you our decision later."

The twins ran outside and sat on the dock by the pond. Swinging their legs above the water, Terrance and Tabitha waited, occasionally smiling at each other. But the time dragged.

Finally the dinner bell rang. The twins ran as fast as they could to the kitchen door and burst into the large farmhouse kitchen.

"Wash your hands and...," began Mom.

"What did you decide? We can't wait! Just tell us!" shouted Terrance.

Animal Lovers (cont.)

"Okay, sit down," said Mom. "Your father and I have discussed your proposal and called Dr. Wong. He feels the two of you are very capable of running this type of operation. And he has faith that you will make wise decisions about handling injured or scared animals. That was one of our big concerns, you two. Not that you couldn't handle the responsibility, but the chance that you might be in danger."

Dad continued, "If we let you try this, it's on a trial basis only, just for the summer months. And you can never have more than six "residents" at a time. You also have to promise that you will try to find good homes for the strays, or to locate their owners."

Tabitha and Terrance couldn't sit still any longer. They flew out of their chairs and hurled themselves at their parents, hugging and kissing them.

Terrance let out a loud, "Hooray!" as he let go of Dad and grabbed his mother around her waist for a squeeze.

"You guys won't regret this," said Tabitha, as she sat down at the dinner table. "We won't let you down."

As Terrance sat down next to Tabitha he asked his sister, "Now what are we going to call this place?"

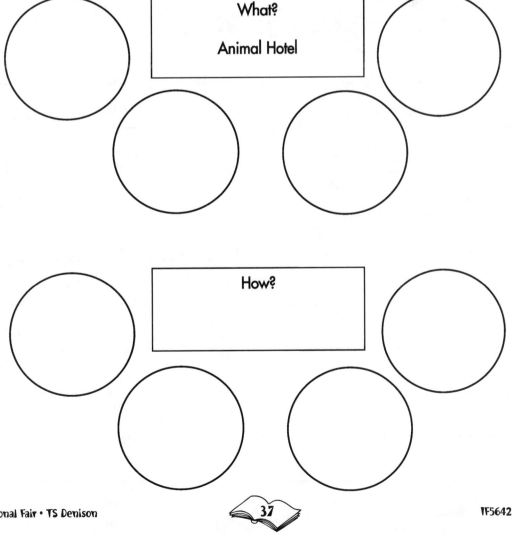

Another Kind of Rhino

Read the report, then answer the questions below.

In the fall of the year, the seeds of the rhino bush are spread, during the migratory movements of the giraffe-necked blackbird. The seeds remain intact until the winter frosts of the Lake Superior watershed thaw. It is only in the iron-enriched soil of this region that the rhino bush grows. As its shoots burst through the earth's surface, the rhino bush emits a powerful odor, much like that of its mammalian namesake. Throughout the summer months, the plant, which is not really a bush but an annual weed, grows quickly and may reach a height of one meter and a circumference of three meters. At three months, its leaves are covered with grayish-green hairy spikes. In the fourth month a series of deep green double flowers appear. It is the nutlike seed of these flowers that so thoroughly tantalizes the appetite of the giraffe-necked blackbird, who will eat vast quantities of the plant. As autumn snows arrive, the cold kills the rhino bush. The soil beneath the plant will be devoid of vegetation for one year.

Now summarize the report by writing short notes of no more than six words per statement. Be sure your facts are written in sequential order.

The Life of a Rhino Bush

I _____

II _____

III _____

IV _____

V _____

VI _____

VII _____

VIII _____

IX _____

X _____

New Tricks

Read the cartoon, then answer the questions below.

1. Write a brief summary of this cartoon.

_____

2. The child dumps her food because ...

_____

3. Circle the term that best describes the story.

mystery   tragedy   science fiction   fantasy   comedy

4. Why do you think so?

_____

_____

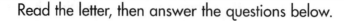

Name _____

A New Jersey

> Read the letter, then answer the questions below.

Dear Grandma,

   Thank you very much for the strikingly vivid soccer jersey you bought for me. I love the flowery pink and orange pattern! But I'm afraid I will be unable to wear it at Saturday's soccer tournament. You see, the team colors are blue and yellow. I guess it's a league thing.

   The jersey is plenty big. Thank you for your thoughtfulness in choosing a size I won't outgrow any time soon. Mom and I estimate I'll get at least four years of use out of the jersey.

   I hope you visit soon! We would love to see you. Then you can come to soccer practice or a game!

Love,

Madeleine

P.S. No, don't worry about buying similar jerseys for the rest of the team. Ms. Hamm, the team's coach, is quite fond of the present team colors.

1. Summarize this letter. State the purpose of the letter in your summary.

   _____

2. What are two of the problems with the jersey?

   _____

   _____

3. How would you suspect Madeleine feels about the jersey?

   _____

Name _____

Downtown Traffic Flow Halted

Read this fictional news article, then answer the questions below.

Traffic came to a halt Saturday at 8:45 a.m. when the traffic light on the corner of Main Street and Division Avenue went on the blink. By the time the county sheriff's department arrived, vehicles were backed up as far as Maple on the west and Larch from the south.

Sheriff Wiggins said, "Must be the worst case of blockage we've seen in twenty-three years. Don't recall anything like it since the funeral of Jay Bob Newton."

The sheriff immediately deputized Debbie Dobson, daughter of Dil and Dorothy Dickinson, to serve as traffic officer until electricity could be restored. Mrs. Dobson, a school crossing guard, has plenty of experience dealing with unruly traffic. "She done real good," praised Betty Bunsen, a local merchant. "Kept traffic going as smooth as silk, don't you know."

Four Corners Electric Company was able to restore power by 4:00 p.m. Age and maintenance deprivation were blamed for the frayed and faulty wiring. Sherm Greer, spokesperson for FCEC, declared, "Ya wanna have nice new wires that don't pull from rotted old poles, ya gotta get more money for our maintenance coverage. It's just that simple."

1. Summarize this news article in one sentence.

   _____

2. Complete the language chart below. The first phrase is done for you.

Phrase	What Is	Why?
on the blink	traffic light	frayed wires
smooth as silk	_____	_____
worst case of blockage	_____	_____
just that simple	_____	_____

3. Write the name of the person that matches each term below.

   local merchant _____   FCEC Spokesperson _____

   traffic officer _____   sheriff _____

Headlines

Match the six headlines below with the appropriate article.

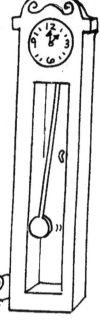

a. Bash Brings Out the Beasts in All
b. Boy's Zeal For Fire Burns Brightly
c. Clock Serves as Pest Control Device
d. Fifth Grade Class—Mutton To Talk About
e. Hairy, Multi-Legged Beast Frightens Girl
f. There's Nothing That a Boy Won't Get Into

_____1. The wooden grandfather clock was about to strike the hour of 1:00 a.m. A small rodent, seeking food, scurried up the facing of the mechanism. When the clockworks whirled and struck the hour, the tiny animal scampered away.

_____2. A prim and proper young lady was seated on a well-cushioned stool in her sitting room. She held a container of yogurt, which she spooned into her mouth ever so daintily. An arachnid lowered itself by its thread to have a good look at this peculiar human, and the prim and proper young lady cried out in horror and vacated the room.

_____3. At the yearly Christmas party, a curious young boy named John had, as the result of ongoing mischief, been required to sit in the corner during the supper hour. There he was fed by his family. When dessert arrived (a fruit tart), John, ever so inquisitive, poked holes into it with his fingers. He speared a fruit on one of his digits and noticing his mother's stern look, cried out, "I'm a good little boy, right, Mommy?"